Swan Song

Selected poems by
Richard Gordon-Freeman

Richard Gordon-Freeman W.

PACKARD PUBLISHING LIMITED

CHICHESTER

For Mary
Fy wrach Gymreig

Swan Song – *Selected poems by Richard Gordon-Freeman*

This edition first published in 2019 by
Packard Publishing Limited, Chichester,
West Sussex, PO19 7LA, UK.

ISBN 978 1 85341 166 3

A CIP record may be obtained from the British Library.

Prepared for press by Michael Packard.
Layout by Hilite Design, Marchwood, Southampton, Hampshire.
Printed and bound in the UK by KnowledgePoint Ltd, Winnersh, Berkshre.

Acknowledgements

Some of the poems in this book have appeared in: *Agenda, Ambit,* the Arts Council's *New Poems, Borderlines, Iota, Orbis, PEN Broadsheet No. 6, PEN Broadsheet No. 8, PEN New Poems 76-77, PEN New Poems 77-78, Poetry Book Society Supplement 1978, Poetry Dimension 1, Poetry Dimension 5, Portfolio Poets, Purple Patch, The French Literary Review, Here Now, The Honest Ulsterman, The Lancet, The Listener, London Magazine, New Statesman, The Times Literary Supplement.*

Some of the poems have been broadcast by the BBC; others were included in the record *London Poets*, produced with the financial help of the Greater London Arts Association.

'Snooker player' was used by the Scottish Examinations Board in a syllabus for English Literature. 'Under the hosepipe' illustrated by Martin Ware, was published in a limited edition by Peter Leigh. 'Swimming: 1949' was a Sycamore Press *Broadsheet*, edited by John Fuller.

Contents

A beer reverie 1
A Chinese soldier in Tibet. 2
A Cranach Adam and Eve 3
A letter to the Alphabet. 4
A pun in French 5
A Zen story 6
Abbey River. 7
A4isms – and more of them . . . . 8 - 11
After the opera 12
All will be revealed. 13
Amazing space. 14
An English walk 15
Apollinaire . . . . 16 - 17
At last we have a letter. 18
At Louisa Lodge, Bedgebury Forest 19
At Sydney cricket ground 20
At the field of gold 21
Big babies. 22
Birdnesting 23
Bird watcher 24
Biro 25
Bloody slippers 26
Bonfire. 27
Canadians. 28
Cannibal poem. 29
Clissold 30
Company medical. 31
Das Ohrwurm. 32
Daynight. 33
Either drink, or depart 34
Emily Rotärmel 35
Face . . . . 36 - 37
Finders keepers losers weepers. 38
Five sentences. 39
Flatmate 40
Flemish proverbs 41

From the Bestiary of Guillaume Apollinaire . . . . 42 - 43
From the Oxford Dictionary of Plays, 2005 44
Gobstoppers 45
Going home . . . . 46 - 47
Guiding lights 48
Hanged man 49
If you're in an American movie 50
In a nosegay garden 51
International art English . . . . 52 - 53
Je fis de Macabré la danse . . . . 54 - 55
Knockout competition 56
Lead soldiers 57
Let the sheep piss 58
Life and death in seven letters 59
Like chess pieces 60
Long division 61
Lunch in Paris 62
Mating frogs 63
Max Ernst . . . . 64 - 65
Mistaken identity 66
My mime 67
Noah 68
Nostalgia . . . . 69 - 70
On the Underground . . . . 71 - 72
Pantechnicon-van 73
Parts . . . . 74 - 76
Pet mice 77
Picnickers 78
Place for a castle 79
Point-to-point 80
Portrait of a gentleman 81
Railway sleepers 82
Rain 83
Remembering my savings stamp 84
Rossini, Senior Crescendo 85
Snooker player 86
Snow 87
Some of those handbags are almost human 88

Stop cock 89
Strangford, Ulster 90
Swimming: 1949 . . . . 91 - 92
Thames; the upper reaches . . . . 93 - 95
That time of year 96
The air man . . . . 97 - 98
The albatross coast – La Côte d'Albâtre 99
The bouquet 100
The cat and the bird 101
The dog's name 102
The drawer 103
The great hat race . . . . .104 - 106
The guard 107
The Irish fiddler 108
The Reverend Robert Walker skating
    on Duddingston Loch, by Sir Henry Raeburn 109
The swan 110
The tinned scream 111
The 218 bus around 1949 . . . . .112 - 113
There are many Niles 114
Things undone 115
Thinks bubbles 116
Three train journeys . . . . .117 - 118
To Mr Hudgell, at May Cottage . . . . .119 - 121
To the red wine stains on the table cloth in a
    French restaurant (1936) 122
Trotting races at Portbail 123
Two ponds . . . . .124 - 125
Two winds 126
Under the hosepipe 127
Virgin and child 128
White-ribbon day 129
Wicket-keeper 130
World War One 131
Written in my room 132

Biography 133

Mars, Venus, Saturn — the amazing thing is not that we discovered these planets, but that we actually know their names.
Emile Cioran

A serious and good philosophical work could be written consisting entirely of jokes.
Ludwig Wittgenstein

The apparent world is the real world and it is occupied by weeds, rubble and vermin.
Friedrich Nietzsche

It may be hard for an egg to turn into a bird, but it would be a jolly sight harder for it to learn to fly while remaining an egg.
C. S. Lewis

A beer reverie

A mole uses the lawn like a swimming pool,
Throwing up brown splashes.
We all come to that.

I swish at a fly with my newspaper,
That tells me an Irish Prime Minister
Cannot distinguish between a bomb
And a bowler hat.

Our postman can.
He knows everything. With a postman
Like him, we don't need letters.

How can a dead bird catch fish?
When a kingfisher's feathers fly
Bound to the fisherman's steel hook.
One question less.

One question more.
Can water be found in a dried-up lake?
Yes: rainwater caught in a grounded boat.

As sure as the A23 goes to Brighton,
As sure as you like making love with the light on,
Sitting quietly, doing nothing,
Will always take you somewhere.

To the refrigerator for another beer,
And there's more technology in the can
Than the whole world knew in Christ's time.

A Chinese soldier in Tibet

To punish the old men for praying
We pulled down their temples,
And smashed each stone to powder
For the wind and rain to carry away.
When foolish men spoke against us

We stripped off their daughters' clothes
And drove them along the busiest roads;
There was looking-but-not-seeing, we know.
The priests were made to kill, to marry,
To work... things I thought no worse

Than being without meat, a woman,
Or money, in this wretched place.
But I have heard a strange thing:
Two pearl-shaped, purple fragments
Of bone, the size of grains of rice,

Each in a tiny, golden bowl,
In five growing-larger boxes,
Were found in a cave near my home.
The Buddha's ashes made eight parts
For eight countries. Seven are lost

But one is found, near my home,
With papers that say in ancient words,
These are the holy Buddha's bones.
One who speaks my language said
That sometime, somewhere, someone

Will take up a basket of river mud
To fill a mould for bricks and make –
Remake – a stone we ground to nothing
And lay it as a new foundation.
Such things I've never heard before.

A Cranach Adam and Eve

A knowing Eve in a most balletic pose
Stands beneath a laden apple tree.
Adam's opposing (in the heraldic sense)
And each fruit on the bough resembles
Eve's small round breasts in size.

The apples are even painted in pairs,
And on each one the calyx is placed
Exactly where the nipple would be.
But if not breasts, then they are eyes,
About to be the first to witness shame.

A letter to the alphabet

Dear Alf I haven't called upon you lately,
Not having much to say, and naturally lazy.
Still it's better to think of nothing
Than not to think at all; better to stare in
To disconcerting darkness than be without sight,
And realise it's poetry that makes life
More interesting than poetry can be.
Poetry, let's say, serves as the offertory
Hymn, bringing unimaginable gifts.
Alf, you got us into this, and it's
An occupation that rarely brings us peace,
Though I'll be happy writing lines like this:
Sometimes the moon's a plate, sometimes a knife.

A pun in French

The weather's been as unreliable as a baby's bum
Although today we've seen a modicum of sun,

So out come the new shoes, bought too hastily
In a sale at a French *supermarché.*

Even when laced as tight as a corset
They feel too big for my impatient feet.

I walk to the corner. People look round when
They hear the flop-flop of a strolling pelican.

In shoes size matters, above style and colour.
I liked this pair, but now I'm not *chaussures*.

A Zen story

Two monks came to a turbulent stream
Where a beautiful woman was waiting.
Without a word, one of them
Took her upon his back and waded
To the other side. His companion
Was astonished at what he had seen,
Remembering their solemn vow
Never to lay hands on a woman.
All day, in silence, they walked on,
Until the other stopped, and bowed,
And dealt him a heavy blow
With his stick, and angrily said,
Why *are you still carrying the load*
That I set down many hours ago?

Abbey river

I hauled my canoe up unused rollers.
White and brown turbans of foam
Stirred and turned, and turned into swans.

Angry, angrier and angriest
Are the usual forms of swan-welcome:
They hissed me like a bad actor.

I passed the cob and two cygnets
And warming to it, soon surprised
The gentler pen, with another youngster.

They turned, paddling hastily away
Along their corridor of anxiety:
From footsteps in a lonely alley.

And I could not overtake them.
They grew tired, tired and distressed,
And by fleeing, made me stop.

Then they slowed, and stopped.
I abandoned the trip, turned; returning
Met the other three, in line-ahead,

Hurrying to unite the family,
Glad to see me go, hissing again,
Shaking their snaky heads.

After the war, when eggs were short,
My brother and I, young and frightened
In a stolen dinghy, took a swan's egg

Which our mother turned
Into three fluffy cakes
That sat on the sideboard like pretty hats.

A4isms

In the summer drink Côtes du Rhône,
And in the winter, Overcoats du Rhône.

Alice in Wonderland is ungrammatical.
A Louse in Wonderland is the correct title.

When captaining a ship be sure to choose
Sailors who can't swim to be your crew,
Who won't sit idly playing with their cocks
While your vessel drifts towards the rocks.

The snail will get to Christmas
At the same time as the rest of us.

Don't be late twice on the same day.
If you were late for work, leave early.

Take the trouble to look for Him
And God may bless you, on a whim.

Perhaps you met the invisible man
As a baby in an empty pram.

Nothing is more obviously missing than morale
In the military, the sporting, and the choral.

Two snowballs make the snowman a snowman,
Two snowballs make the snowwoman a snowwoman.

Most people die having committed less than murder.
It's a pity, but that's the way things are.

Growing old is falling asleep in the sun
And waking up in cold rain.

Sighs by the sea-side
Take on the size of the sea.

Nobody knows where a secret passage is.
That's why they're called secret passages.

Sometimes if you need a police car
It's quicker by far to ring for a pizza.

Religion's dream or revolution's nightmare?
Don't move. Stay just where you are.

It's pitch dark at the base of the lighthouse.
If you want to see, don't stand too close.

You can't buy a mullet
With a sardine in your pocket.

Anarchists chalk up the letter A
Everywhere they go.
Why? Because it's the only letter they know.

All would be well
If we all thought like Orwell.

More A4isms

The mnemonic for Monique
Is Mnemonique

Though he writes with a Biro,
His poetry is not Byronic.

The alpha male and the alpha female
Make love in the alphabed.

Murder is only a crime for seven years.
Then we set you free
And bring your victim back to life.

How different they were,
Those two choir-boys,
Haydn and Hitler.

Looking for something new
Is the oldest pastime in the world,
So look for something new.

Too many people work in the factory
Where the only thing they make
Is mistakes.

At Bournemouth the waves of the sea
Had an English correctness, said Debussy.

Different latitudes,
Same platitudes.

In a police state,
The police are also
In a police state.

If a lovely woman whispers in his ear
I'm not wearing any underwear
Even the most faithful husband
Will shed a rueful tear.

Some poets are to drink
As some little girls are to pink.

Call your dog bow-wow,
Call your cat miaou,
Call your canary tra-la-la,
Call McGuinness a mur-der-er.

You are defined by the people you admire,
Unless you are a liar and say you admire liars.

Renounce all vices like Walter of Gloucester
And throw the backgammon set into the cess pit.

It's not the first kiss you remember, it's
The first kiss with lipstick.

Zorro had to wear a mask
In order to be recognised.
No one had to ask.

After the opera

It isn't over until the fat lady
Stops singing, the massive curtain
Falls, and her ghost, all lah-di-
Dah, comes out to make certain

You leave. The slovenly orchestra
Steal their instruments and make for
A nearby, late-night bar.
You shuffle towards the fire-door,

Out into an unseasonable heat,
Leaving your slippery programme
Unwanted by the tipped-up seat.
You're confused when the wrong man

Takes your arm at the kerb-side,
Whispering things you don't understand;
But in no language has he ever lied
About the performance you must attend.

Step out over the puddle of fire,
Following his twisted stride
Into that unimaginable nowhere
That we shall all so easily find.

All will be revealed

It's always a surprise to see your name
On a seating-plan, a short list, a team-sheet,
Or held aloft by a uniformed chauffeur
At the airport or railway station.

Mine was painted in coarse green letters
On an MDF board leaning by the roadside
Up ahead.
FREE
MAN
Summoning me to a pit stop
In a race I didn't know I was in.

Placards and graffiti demanding
FREE MANDELA
Always caused a jolt of recognition,
Like unexpectedly catching your reflection
In a shop window, say.

When I drew level with the home-made sign
I could see the message in full.
It said
FREE
MANURE.

Amazing space

When the Mona Lisa was stolen from the Louvre
More people went to see the empty space
Than viewed the picture on a normal day.
Such is the power of curiosity.
Visitors gazed at the wall, not her painted face,
And strolled to a nearby café to talk it over.

An English walk

You can walk
From Hants to Wilts
To Berks to Bucks
To Herts to Beds
To Cambs to Hunts
To Lincs to Notts
And walk back
From Notts to Lincs
To Hunts to Cambs
To Beds to Herts
To Bucks to Berks
To Wilts to Hants

Apollinaire

Father might have been a Roman priest,
Though everyone calls *them* father, or possibly
The Bishop of Monaco. It's complicated, like spaghetti.
Strongest candidate is Francesco-Costantino-Camillo Flugi
d' Aspermont. A Swiss-Italian. An aristocrat at least.

Mother was Angelica de Kostrowitsky, a Finnish-
Born lady of Polish origin with Russian nationality.
She christened her Roman-nosed son over-enthusiastically:
Wilhelm Albert Vladivar Alexandre Apollinaris. Me.
I took the name Guillaume Apollinaris. It has a flourish.

Briefly, we lived in Monaco, Cannes, Nice; casino cities.
When I grew up, I went to live in Paris, aged twenty,
Just over half-way through my life. Then to Germany,
In 1901, as a tutor, where I fell in love with the nanny,
An English girl called Annie Playden. More's the pity,

Because this Finnish-Polish-Russian-Italian-Swiss
French-resident went to London twice to propose;
Twice too often for Miss Playden. My Roman nose
Failed in the tragedy and comedy of goodbyes and hellos,
But sniffed out the painters to do the century's business.

In 1911 I was arrested on suspicion of stealing the Mona Lisa
From the Louvre, as if I wanted to get my mother back!
I spent a week in prison, a week for that nicknack,
When I'd Delaunay, Matisse, Picasso and Braque
As friends – fresh ideas, new canvasses. I was their priest, the

Man who spoke for them. In 1913 I moved into 2002
Boulevard St. Germain. Then came the war.
I enlisted, which earned me French citizenship the following year.
To most people's annoyance, I felt no fear,
War was a beautiful thing, beautifully new.

I wrote *The sky is starry with Bosch shells;*
The marvellous forest where I live is giving a ball.
Soon after I became French, a piece of shrapnel
Took up residence in my head. They trepanned my skull
To remove the splinter. But you can never tell

What's round the next corner. I survived long enough
To marry Jacqueline Korb, a pretty red-head,
(Like me, during my operation). Picasso, another red,
Was a witness. After six months of happiness, I was dead,
Carried off by Spanish flu, a surrealist to the end. (*Cough.*)

At last we have a letter

At last we have a letter from our son
Who's journeying in a southerly direction
Across Mexico and the Amazon. He rambles on
For pages. Unfortunately I dropped them
In the hall, so the narrative has become
Random in places. He makes a confession,
Says he's stuck his cock into a man!
No clues are given as to the location
Of this event. It was a difficult penetration.
He tried verso and recto, and had his fun
In the end, but I may have got it wrong –
His writing wriggles like a hooked worm.
I have re-read his long description
Of the clothes this man may have worn.
He had a white shirt and a black jacket on,
Was short, stiff-necked, seemed to be sitting down,
And particularly maladroit when trying to turn.
Such awful writing, such confusion.
It's possible his bed-mate was a nun,
But I prefer to think a kind of penguin.

At Louisa Lodge, Bedgebury Forest

I.
To amuse visiting children, I did the egg trick:
Bowled an innocent egg over the chimney
To land intact on grass. Evolution has planned
For laying on the wing, eggs tumbled from nests,
And saved the egg when it hit gigantic Earth.
But lost patience that we should test it twice.
There, cried the boy, hurling the egg at a wall,
There, it's not unbreakable at all.

2.
The well kept even temperatures below its rotting cover,
Was never warm or frozen over. The shaft confused the eye;
A watched bucket filled cloudily, and the attentive ear
Also drew unclear water. A crooked, rusty arm
Wound the thirst in tight. Each link of the chain
Shone like a throat. My child lifted her face
Reflected in water, in catch-a-ball hands,
And threw it in the air, shattering with laughter.

3.
At near-dark, when the shadow slipped into the body,
The path, like a diary, told you where to go.
From never-breathed air, between the pines, I raised
Birds who needlessly flew to identical trees.
For miles, nothing but silent palisades
Thinning out to hop-poles with high wires.
Only the owl, Hughie's Mum, had a voice.
Hughie, Hughie! She called, but he never came.

At Sydney Cricket Ground

The players look like thawing snowmen,
The ball unwinds its endless geometry.
There are more beer cans than people
And some of them are learning how to fly.
A beer-sweat glazes the crowd, a sameness,
Something of a captured army, fallen-out,
Relaxing in a sketch-book of sullen poses.
Even their freckles resemble tiny Australias.
When the sun flashes from a lens
Just behind the opposite boundary fence
Only a lunatic would think of a gun
In this land of uninterrupted peace.
Just the same, one of the fielders drops,
Hit by the ball in the region of the heart.
Every game is part of a larger game –
For a moment, two games overlapped.
The victim is led tottering off the pitch;
The fast bowler resumes his cracking pace,
Although he's troubled by a nagging stitch,
And the old spectator polishes his glasses.

At the field of gold
For Clare

We stood before a five-barred gate
Twice the height of you,
With a broken sign on display:
Beware of the B, and a U...

With loving hands I lifted you up
And asked what you thought it meant.
You said *Beware of the buttercups,*
The perfect reply for the moment.

Big babies

The mother-truck parks, clanking scaffolding,
Followed by big babies in a smoky van
That blares pop music from Radio Something.

We watch the open-mouthed generation
Erect its climbing frame, spit and swear,
And warming up as the job gets swiftly done

Pull off their out-grown T-shirts to bare
Tattoos as complex as any Celtic art.
They know we hate them, and they don't care.

When the pretty, young au pair walks past
The big babies want her to notice them.
Want her. She falters, and looks aghast

At the howls and groping gestures from the pen.
She stares vaguely away, lonely and afraid;
This, they think, is what really makes them men.

Birdnesting

High up in our village Himalayas
Were eggs delicately painted in watercolours.
We carried stolen eggs in our hot mouths,
Leaving our hands free for climbing down.
An egg-collection was a kind of bank account,
Swapped for other things that you might want.

We all obeyed the serious boyish rules
Of birdnesting, knew that birds were fools
Unable to count higher than two, therefore
We only robbed a clutch of three or more.
The eggs were emptied by making a hole each end
And blowing the contents out onto the ground.

It always looked as though you were being sick,
Bent over like that, lips puffing at an egg.
An addled egg was left in the flower-bed
With a larger hole, to let the ants get
In, and eat away the golden bird
Inside. We understood the ways of the world.

Some eggs were superstitiously left alone:
All the owls, the robin and the wren
Were protected by our grumpy little gods,
Lords of the rain-beetles and death's-head moths,
Of dragonflies and ladybirds... I could not
Kill one of these now, even for a bet.

I would have to pay with a mouthful of feathers,
The hatched, guilty, unswallowable taste that has
Nothing to do with common sense. For we
Have to be choosy about our cruelties.
Older, I think it's right that kids should not
Be allowed to blow an egg's brains out.

Bird watcher

Where a fallen tree
Strikes grey lightning
Into the water, three
Death-gazing coots
Have cornered a duck.

She trails a wing
Like a hank of hair
Slipped from its pins.

In the unnatural silence
Of things brought closer
Through binoculars
The coot's nature
Is without music or colour.

Black suits their work,
And soon they will drown her.

They pickaxe her head
Patiently. If the meek
Inherit the earth
It will be like this,
By the mouthful.

Near my ticking wrist
A butterfly's wings close
Like a spring-trap
On their own beauty.

Biro

When the first Biro arrived
In our village
People used to knock
On the owner's door and ask
If they could see it work.

He showed how it wrote under water,
And upside-down, and let them run
Their finger over the ballpoint–
The exciting new oxymoron!

So no more crossed nibs,
And almost smudge-free ink.
Men asked for one for their birthdays,
Or for Christmas.
It did what an Osmiroid or Watermans
Pen couldn't do, but at a stroke
Their writing became worse.

Bloody slippers

My friend arrived in Austria
Like a man falling off a chair,
Startling the green soldiers
Who grow along such borders.
They found him brandy, kicked the fire,
Kept an eye on *over there*
And fetched a yawning officer
To get the details down on paper.
Hungarian? How old? How far?
He looked as if he'd walked a year.
They cut his jammed laces, poured
Blood from his boots, found a pair
Of slippers that he kept as a souvenir.
When he celebrates the day the wire
Drew back its claws, he leaves his door
Open, and welcomes all-comers
In his frayed, blood-stained slippers.

Bonfire

The tortoise had a shell
Of dirty playing-cards
Dropped in a heap,

Blear eyes, an old bone
For a head, loose legs.
She hid in piled leaves,

Only stirring when they'd burnt
Down to soft, grey ashes.
Almost too hot to touch,

She edged towards the flower-bed,
And went through her own funeral.
But a few days later,

Clambered out again, uncovering
Papery, unfertilised eggs.
I watch her creep along the wall,

The creature of the bone-fire,
The heart of phoenix
Stuck in an ugly stool.

Canadians

Tugs push white moustaches across
Placid water in the London docks.

We mount the gangplank, steep as a chute,
And check in to a brisk salute.

Astern they fly a maple leaf
As large as a king-size double sheet.

The entire Italian polo team
Couldn't match these sailors' charm.

We're not sure who we are, Ma'am,
But we know we're not American.

Waiters offer trays and fill
Glasses: men who are trained to kill.

Yes Sir, we're a bilingual fish,
We can kill in French or English.

Cannibal poem

Has anyone ever eaten a cuckoo,
Or a cuckoo and a cockatoo too,
Or a cockatoo followed by a cuckoo or two,
Or two cockatoos followed by a cuckoo,
Or two cuckoos followed by two cockatoos?
Do you remember that German cannibal?
He was cuckoo and he ate a cock or two.

Clissold

The farm's name is wrapped in *Cold;*
Frost blurs everywhere the eye can see.
No hint, in the white on white, of any
Living thing; the valley is on hold.

We bucket water up for the hacks,
Past the rotting mound of straw
And muck, then slither down for more.
Up there and back, up and back...

I hobble the trace of a summer path,
Leaving the other to manage the hay,
And by the stream that pours away
Down-hill, attempt some clumsy maths

About moving water. In that half-hour,
While the frost ebbed an inch on the lawn,
How much was carried up, flowed down:
Were we a hundred, a thousand times slower?

The thaw may come in a few silver days,
And the frozen stable-yard tap run clear.
Indoors, I yawn-in the New Year,
Worn out by the farm's old, slow ways.

Company medical

I handed the nurse my specimen, in a washed-out Nescafé jar.
I'd nothing else to put it in, I apologised to her.
She asked me to sit down.
The doctor's a little late;
He doesn't live in town, but you won't have long to wait.

The doctor looked like death, and his hands were shaking.
As he placed them on my chest, I heard wind breaking.
So you're off to foreign parts?
Lucky man! He said.
I never get further than Barts. He sadly shook his head.

In minutes, it was over. I buttoned up my coat.
He wasn't very thorough. He hadn't looked down my throat.
I thought of raging cholera,
Of dengue fever and shivers,
Of rabies and malaria, and worms that eat your liver,

Of typhoid, smallpox and other things that I couldn't name,
But he just looked me over, with medical disdain.
He knew what I was thinking,
And spoke from the depths of his chair;
If you're fit to work in London, you're fit to work anywhere.

Das Ohrwurm

There is no off-switch for the music I hear
All day until I sleep, that strikes up again
On waking, ghost music that needs no ear
Or apparatus, whose origin is in the brain.

Nor is the selection in my hands;
The music persists without sequence or theme.
Soloists, groups, orchestras and bands
Take their turns until silenced by a dream –

And would return, even if I turned deaf.
The saint's or the god's, Cecilia's or Apollo's
Curse, muttered under sacred breath,
Was *He shall have music wherever he goes*.

Daynight

I close the shutters one by one,
As if pictures of the garden,
And of the vines, are being taken down
And stored outside.

Darkness fits the house perfectly,
From wall to wall and floor to ceiling.
The house has closed
Its eyes, and my eyes.

I've made a long night on a hot afternoon
By turning the wooden pages,
By fiddling with latches, bars and bolts.
Even the sounds of the night return:

Water twisting in a pipe somewhere,
An imagined footfall outside the door.
But nothing will enter except
Thunder and the hunters' fusillades.

All done, we drive away
Through the deserted vineyards,
And disappear like a fly
In folds of green corduroy.

Either drink, or depart

Harvesters bow stiffly to vines
They will dance with for a fortnight.
Girls still wear the *Kiss-me-not,*
Named by the English centuries
Ago, that all shrewd mothers
Made their daughters wear,
To keep off soldiers and the sun,
But for how long? Wine came
With Latin and a previous army –
The grapes are notes in a song.
They give secretive, black wine
That is put back underground
To learn civility. The vines must suffer,
Are pruned hard, leaving two branches
To bear fruit. These older vines
Make better wine, but little of it;
When this vintage is drinking,
They'll have been uprooted and burnt.
Aut bibat, aut abeat, wrote Cicero:
You must either drink or depart.
Inevitably, we shall do both,
And great wines made by the father
Will be enjoyed by the son.

Emily Rotärmel

Her lips were as red as the shiny button you push
To start machinery, her overdone tan
Applied by the sun at ski resorts and lidos.

Her black hair had the grey rinsed away
With the past. When we whispered on the landing
In our dressing gowns sex loomed like a breaker.

Definitions of virginity don't exist –
She was my first, I was probably her worst,
But got by in her tongue enough to understand
When she said *Have you let one go*?

Her name meant Little Red Arms. There was blood
On my hands from the lab. where we worked.

Emily's arms were as warm as a scarf,
And she explained how the young men
Of her age had disappeared during the war,
And never returned. All her life her lovers
Were a generation older, until I came along.

On hot days she wore only underwear
Under her spotless lab-coat. I watched the eyes
Of the *Herr Doktors* follow her, and I had seen her
Naked, smiling her bright-red smile.

Face

This silver-fish on my middle finger's
Eleven years younger than the rest of me,
The result of an accident with a pen-knife
Belonging, appropriately, to the butcher's boy.
Auditing my scars reminds me of friendships.
On the right arm, are faint telegraph wires
Where pieces of glass from the smashed windows
Of a car scratched an insignificant warning.
Stretched around my left leg
Like a rubber band is a wide cicatrice
Dubbed by a nail in a rugby boot.
How manly it felt at the time
To be wearing that red garter!
And down my stomach, the institutional cut,
A badly written piece of history
Where a shaky surgeon opened me up
To oust a Quisling piece of gut.
And what looks like a bullet wound –
Was as bloody and almost as dangerous –
Is this hard, round, persistent core
On the left shoulder, where a swollen
Carbuncle burst. Similar poison
Killed poor Wilhelm Grimm.

And now I remember small, blind Jimmy.
His whole head was a scar,
As crude as a hurriedly peeled potato.
He left his looks in a flaming aircraft,
And immigrated here from death.
When we were drinking in The Cricketers
People turned their faces away,
The worry in their smoky eyes
Searching for their children outside.
Some of the things we overheard,
(Because Jimmy could hear with his scar),
Made him lug his coat collar higher.
Then he smiled, I think, and made
Some joke about his ears burning.

Finders keepers losers weepers

In peacetime Syria she unearthed
An unusual flat-cast joined figurine
From the second millenium BC,
While in Sicily her team found the smooth
Marble statue of a young satyr,
A rough goatskin draped on his shoulders.
In Saqqara she discovered the tomb
Of a high-ranking government official
Of the nineteenth dynasty.
But her most exciting find
Was the divorced history teacher
She picked up on a hen night
Who gave her more pleasure
Than if she'd gazed on the gold mask
Of Agamemnon in his Mycenaean tomb.

Five sentences

BARDOLPH: Why sir, for my part,
I say the gentleman
had drunk himself out of his five sentences.

EVANS: It is 'his five senses.'
Fie, what the ignorance is!

One. It is important to know
When to think and when not to think.

Two. It is important to know
What to say and what not to say.

Three. It is important to know what
Others will think.

Four. It is important to know
What others will say.

Five. Luther said you are not only responsible
For what you say, but also for what you do not say.

Flatmate

Some evenings he studiously fiddled
Under a standard lamp in the corner
With the cigarettes he would take
To work next day,
Prodding and poking with a needle
Like the cross-legged tailor
In the fairy story.

He was a hard-up trainee
In the advertising world,
Tormented by girls he couldn't afford
To lunch at Bianchi's, Leoni's or L'Escargot.
He could never lay a finger on them,
But could use his finger to point out
The girls who had unknowingly
Smoked one of his pubic hairs.

Flemish proverbs

Brueghel with his story-telling eyes
Honoured the country people he knew and loved,
For they had common-sense down to an art

In proverbs nodded through *nem. con.* Approved!
They knew the tiles on their roofs weren't pies,
That cheats are sometimes given the best cards,

That a beautiful plate is worthless without food,
That some shear sheep and some take shears to pigs,
That a fish can be caught by hand, from another's purse,

And if there's a fool in the house, there's probably two,
That horse-droppings are not lush ripe figs,
And you can fire a second bolt to find the first,

That no good comes from confessing to the devil,
And that after you've been taught how to steal
You have to learn how to be hanged as well.

From the Bestiary of Guillaume Apollinaire

The carp
In your pools and your fish-ponds,
You carp seem to live so long!
Fish of such deep melancholy,
Death has forgotten you – slowly.

The Octopus
Squirting ink towards the sky,
Sucking the blood of his lady-
Love and finding it delicious, why,
This monster sounds like me.

The cat
What I want in my house
Is a woman with common sense,
A cat tip-toeing its way
Through the books, and friends.
Without all these, I'd call it a day.

The mouse
Beautiful days, the mice of time,
Bit by bit you nibble my life away.
God, I'll soon be twenty-nine!
I've wasted my life, I'm happy to say.

The crayfish
Oh how I love you, indecision,
You and me, cumbersome and slow.
When we need to change our position,
Like the crayfish, backwards we go.

The caterpillar
Hard work leads to riches;
So, poor poets, scribble away.
The caterpillar who works *sans cesse*
Will be a butterfly one day.

The locust
Look at the delicate locusts,
The wilderness food of John the Baptist.
If only my poems could be like them,
Tit-bits enjoyed by famous men.

From the Oxford Dictionary of Plays, 2005

(Theobald) is outraged because his wife Louise accidentally dropped her bloomers while watching the Kaiser's procession.

Jack is now alarmed because he has become impotent, and demands his penis back from Alice.

Eventually the doll gets stuck up the engineer's rear, causing him to explode.

(Ida) leaves quickly when (Victor) demands she fart for him.

Mum soliloquises about masturbating a young stranger in the cinema, only to discover when the lights come on that it is Mike.

Ian masturbates, tries to strangle himself, weeps, laughs, hugs the dead soldier, digs out the baby's body (and) eats it…

(Solomon) puts on a 'laughing' record and begins to laugh 'with tears in his eyes'.

The Penguin version excludes the disco-owner Marco but names him in the cast list.

(John) Godber became aware that most theatre productions are tedious and intended for middle-class audiences.

Gobstoppers

We are the sugar-babies who opened wide
To curly spoonfuls of molasses, treacle and honey,
To fruity syrup-of-figs, and sugar lumps
After face-pulling medicine. We sucked on
Humbugs, gobstoppers, barley-sugar sticks
And lemon sherberts, the sweetest of all sweets.

Later we laced our cups of tea and coffee
With the light-catching white and brown granules,
The false friends, it seems; the fatteners, the killers.
But that's not why we're bitter now we're older.
Let's spell it out. It's because we cannot say
What we want. Gobstoppers are here to stay.

Going Home
After Jacques Prévert

This Breton returns to his land of birth
Having made a lot of mistakes in life
He wanders past the factories at Douarnenez
He doesn't recognise anyone
Nobody recognises him
He is very sad.
He goes into a crêperie to eat some crêpes
But he can't eat them
There's something that stops them going down
He pays
He leaves
He lights a cigarette
But he can't smoke it.
There is something
Something in his head
Something not right
He gets sadder and sadder
And suddenly he begins to remember:
Someone said to him when he was small
You will end up on the scaffold
And over the years
He never dared do anything
Not even put out to sea
Not even cross the road
Nothing absolutely nothing.
He remembers.
The chap who made that prediction was uncle Grésillard
Uncle Grésillard who wished ill to the whole world
The bastard!

And the Breton thinks of his sister
Who works at Vaugirard
Of his brother killed in the war
Thinks of everything he has seen
Everything he has done.
He is overcome by sadness
He tries once again
To light a cigarette
But he doesn't feel like smoking
Then he decides to go and see uncle Grésillard.
He goes there
He opens the door
Uncle doesn't recognise him
But he recognises his uncle
And he says
Bonjour oncle Grésillard
And then he breaks his neck.
And he ends up on the scaffold at Quimper
After eating half-a-dozen crêpes
And smoking a few cigarettes.

Guiding lights

At night a yellow, oblong moon
Balances on the horizon of the dunes.
Friends and passers-by all agree
That it's a window, a window definitely.
In daytime if you stand on the same spot
You can see it's not a window, definitely not.
There's nothing there, no houses, no trees,
Only rumpled dunes hiding the sea.

In the opposite direction, the lighthouse
Too is a nightlight, built on an enormous
Cliff, twirling its beams. First pointlessly
Over the fields, then searching the sea,
Half useful, half wasted, like charity.
If the window exists, it exists only nightly,
Guiding something from somewhere
To a home that isn't always there.

Hanged man

The man they hanged from a sturdy bough
Was in due course proved innocent,
And entitled to a Christian interment,
With prayers to raise his soul from below.

A civic document was required.
The clerc licked his pen with a let-me-see.
He prayed for guidance, and inspired
Wrote that the recently deceased
Had been found dead under a tree.

If you're in an American movie

You quit bars, leaving your drink
Unfinished, and toss down the right bill
To cover the check you haven't looked at.

You suspect people with unusual hobbies,
Such as growing orchids or playing the organ
In ruined chapels. Your best friend is dummer

Than you, his wife, his mother, or any child
With a brace on its teeth. If a soldier shows
A photo of his girl to his new buddies,

The chances are he isn't going to make it.
Attractive women are usually wearing underwear
When they hear an intruder breaking in,

And instead of locking the door and calling the cops,
They begin to search the house diligently.
Nobody takes a shower without having sex

Or getting murdered. Dogs cutely roll their heads
To one side. Old men limp, and hoik their pants
Aggressively. There will be Christmas, with snow.

What you see is as familiar as life itself,
But nothing like it. Wherever you go, the waves
Of music resemble tunes you already know.

In a nosegay garden

Plants to cook with, to freshen the air,
To remedy ills and make scented posies
That pleased the nose or warded off disease
Are laid out formally for bowing inspection.

Pellitory was chewed for the toothache,
Hound's-tongue, to heal bites of mad dogs,
Looks the part. A sympathetic medicine.

A spoonful of seeds of yellow-horned poppy
Loosened the belly greatly, and modest balm
Drove away all melancholy and sadness.

This clump is comfrey-with-the-knobbly-root,
Given to drink against pain in the back
Through wrestling, or over-much use of women.

Cures and care for the sick or miserable
Found in a pretty garden of wise plants,
Providing physic, poultice, and pomander,
(The pills we take today like packets of seeds).

International art English (I didn't write a word of this)

Behind space there was nothing
and in front of it there was no possibility
of escape to anything else.
What you see is not what you see,
and what you see is not what it means.

We leave the solid ground
of rationally categorised experience
and are made immediately aware
of the existence of our own selves.
Such works stimulate the visual
imagination by appealing simultaneously
to our sense of objective proportions
in order to propagate the rediscovery
of elementary imagination
calling in to question the modular elements
of scale, size and volume, and examining the notions
of repetition and duplication in the details.
The employment of actual, everyday
objects serves to augment the reality content
and our ability to enter contemplatively
into the illusion of depth and motion
induced by deceptively simple means.
By concentrating on the unreality
of the canvas or painting surface
canvases could be described
as variations on the theme of infinity.

Speed and improvisation imply
human self-imprisonment
in the adamant edifice of civilisation,
an opportunity to raise the sphere
of the trivia to the status of art
and at the same time to deal
with issues of identity, especially
that of the identity of an object
with its depiction devoid of image
yet dealing entirely with the visual.
The narration and personal content
make this work a powerful commentary
On the human condition.

Je fis de Macabré la danse

The Prince rides out to music, songs and shouts
Of praise. They run to see their Lord
In complete and splendid array, in panoply!

His followers of every rank are costumed
As is fit, as in a lurid masque
With nervous, quarrelsome players;
Men with hot heads and hot-hearts.

Their lives are ruled by opposites;
Despair or joy, cruelty or pious tenderness,
Good or evil, dark or light,
Silence or all sounds all at once.

Woven closely in to this is love
Of symbols. Roses red and white
Tangled with thorns are the blood
Of martyrs and a virgin's purity.

For want of public cruelty
The worthies of the town have bought
A brigand from a nearby place
To watch him butchered,

Sliced in two and each half halved.
The Prince rides there. On either side
His people see but half his face,
As if quartering of the prince himself

Took place. No matter what his station,
Walk or ride, noble or below the low,
A skeleton will dance to each man's side,
Each mortal hand will be taken,

And then the grinning piper will pipe up
Who has no bags for breath, and death
Will drop them all into the earth.

Knockout competition

The draw for the knockout competition
Is pinned to the club's green baize
Notice-board: thirty-two names, a column
That halves when each round's done:
Thirty-two, sixteen, eight, four, two, one.
The winner's name appears half-a-dozen
Times. The notice is displayed for days,
Looking like a family tree cut down.

Lead soldiers

My little men had painted uniforms.
Some dressed in kilts, some khaki battledress,
Some Napoleon's regalia: white trousers worn

With blue tail-coat and tall black shako.
Unfortunately, if handled roughly,
Their feeble necks broke easily, and although

You could straighten a bent sword or rifle,
When a soldier's head came off
We had no magic glues for invisible

Repairs. We knew what to do instead.
You took a matchstick, broke off
Its head and replaced it with your soldier's head,

Then pushed the wooden shaft into
The hollow torso. The beheaded was re-headed,
Ready to fight another Waterloo.

It was as if your wounded man had grown
A quality he hadn't had before –
What the old campaigners called 'backbone'.

Let the sheep piss

The boss was vaccinated with vinegar.
He called me Arthur and all that tralala,
Farting higher than his bony arse,
And shoved granny into the nettles.
I stood there with the blood of a turnip.

Usually I'd just buy a baby without arms
To drink on the park bench, but joined
The terrace lords instead, for a cup of hat juice,
Followed by a Chinaman's leg.
I was well and truly in the cabbages.

Sooner or later we all swallow
Our birth certificates and start
Sucking dandelions by the roots,
So why spend a lifetime sodomising flies?

When the asparagus growers appeared
I recognised a girl amongst them
Who had a crowd on the balcony.

(I'm not interested in a breadboard
With eyes like a fried whiting
Who enjoys it *à la bourgeoise*.)

I knew she travelled by sail or steam,
But I didn't care; I just wanted to fire
My crossbow. She came over and asked
If I'd like to take my little boy to the circus.

No second invitation needed.
When I emptied the cruets,
My toes spread like a bouquet of violets,
While she pretended she was seeing angels.

Life and death in seven letters

Now here
No where

Like chess pieces

Princes in windy cobbled squares
Stand on strange languages and dates
One gesturing 'I will build a city here'
Another 'My army will soon be at their gates'.
None smiles and none truly convinces.

These are actors and the sculptor cannot do
Their acting for them, only shorten a nose,
Corset a paunch, bolster a weak chin.
Their tailors provided no end of finery
But in stone or bronze this fails to impress.
They provide one small, lasting service:
When you are strolling late or lonely,
Their squares are never completely empty.
If nothing else, they provide a kind of company.

Long division

Before the French Revolution, Paris
Was divided between the rich and the poor.

After the first Commune, the Terror, the Convention,
The Directory, the Committee of Public Safety,

After the Consulate, the first Empire, the Restoration,
The Revolution of 1830, the Revolution of 1848,

After the Second Republic, the Second Empire,
The Franco-Prussian War, the Third Republic,

After the Siege of Paris, the Second Commune,
The First World War, the Popular Front,

After the Second World War, and the Fourth Republic,
Paris was still divided between the rich and the poor.

Lunch in Paris

Is that really the Opéra de la Bastille?
We ask passers-by. Apparently it is,
A drab pre-war department store,
A securely-locked pile of unfriendliness.
Therefore a consolation lunch on the pavement,
Where we can pull faces at the façade.

A woman appears on the sunlit public stage,
With thin, prowling energy, whose look
Suggests a touch of madness. Her pianist's
Hand is poised to snatch food from the outer
Tables. Diners pretend to ignore her. She prowls
Closer and in a flash she snatches

A ribbon of ham, crams one end in her mouth
And tosses her head around, devouring it
Like a cormorant swallowing an eel. Off again,
She grabs a handful of pasta from a plate,
But the waiter is closing in. He catches her
Full in the face with water from a jug.

The shock works. Angrily shaking her head,
She withdraws to stroke wet hair from her cheeks.
The ham-eater has pushed his food away,
The pasta-girl is walking off; the waiter's
Gone to fetch another jug of water.
The Opéra de la Bastille. What a disaster!

Mating frogs

The morning's display
Of dog turds stretched
Along the road. Impossibly
Some were moving. There,
And there; look closer:
Fork-lift trucks, loading eyes

Genus *Rana,* precipitated
From clouds of spawn,
As flecks, then wriggling pins,
Then cannibal tadpoles,
Then froglings – cantabile
In water. The males

Were rucksacking tightly
To females twice their size,
Wasting their squat assent
On the drying pavement.
I love them, like wet sand
Held in the open palm.

Some died under treads
Of tyres; desiccated in the sun
To creatures of a shadow play.
Their empty skins, unnaturally
Entire, drifted in the breeze.
In good time, new tadpoles

Will craze the dim pictures
In our local ponds,
Their busy heads and tails
Like the nubs and shadows
Along the edges of pieces
Of an unfinished jigsaw puzzle.

Max Ernst

The day after the first of April in 1891
I hatched from an egg my mother had laid
In an eagle's nest, which the bird brooded
Over for seven years. That's true, and not true.
When I was seven my favourite cockatoo died
The moment my sister was born. Consequently
I became confused between people and birds.

Father taught deaf-mutes, and was a Sunday painter.
I attended the University at Bonn, which rhymes with Saigon,
And organised the first Dada exhibition, in Cologne.
The way to the show was through a public urinal,
Where eau-de-cologne splattered by the bucket-full.
We offered our visitors axes to attack the exhibits.
I served as an artillery engineer in the First World War,

And was wounded, and was wounded, twice. In the head.
Once by a recoiling gun, one of our own guns;
Once by the kick of a mule, one of our own, unpatriotic
Mules. My comrades called me *eisenkopf*, iron-head.
In 1918 I married Louise Strauss, Assistant
To the Director of the Wallraf-Richartz Museum
In Cologne. That starter-marriage ended in 1921.

(Which rhymes with Saigon). In 1922 I slipped
Into France without any papers or money,
To the house of poet Paul Eluard. We had faced
Each other in the endless trenches. I found work
In a factory making cheap souvenirs for tourists,
As minuscularly prophetic as a forgotten dream.
Paul, employed by his father, was our household's
Main support until he stole money from his dad
For a trip overseas. I sold some of Paul's possessions

So that I could meet him in Saigon. His dad forgave him,
Never speaking again of the cash that vanished on the way
To the bank. Paul hated capitalism, but hated even more
The people who didn't hate capitalism as much as him.
We fluttered along; birds of a feather. In '27 I married again,

To Marie-Berthe Aurenche, without her mother's permission.
Unsettled, in 1938 I moved to a house in the Ardèche
With Leonora Carrington, an aristocratic English woman.
She went crazy and sold our house, (it was near Avignon,
Which rhymes with Saigon), for a bottle of brandy.
She was traced to an institution in Spain. I was also interned
In the Second World War, a harmless German put to work

In a factory, making bricks this time. After my labours
The French authorities planned to deport me,
To work on the scorching railways of North Africa.
I also escaped to Spain, and in '41 met Peggy Guggenheim.
I adventurously flew to New York, and married her there.
I left her in 1943 for a painter called Dorothea Tanning,
But the scandal forced us to live in scorching Arizona.

Had major exhibitions in Paris, New York, Cologne; married
Dorothea in '46; returned to France with her in '53 and finally
Became French in 1958, supplementing my four marriages
With three nationalities, and finally died, an old bird
Of eighty-five years. Now you know how things turned out,
You must heartily wish you could have been me, M.E.,
And lived an artist's life that's never been improved on.

Mistaken identity

Our French town is putting on its annual fête:
A Channel Island band, a straggling parade,
Some shy, some show-off children, in fancy dress.
We applaud, wave, pick the one that's best.

The finest figure is the Green Bean, the *haricot vert,*
Walking beside his sister and older brother,
(A carrot and an onion), ushered by their mother.
Heads together, the worthy judges confer.

They announce the third place, then second,
And each youngster is given a polite hand.
The winner is named. We mishear. We cheer.
But up steps an English schoolboy, *'arry Potter*.

My mime
After Raymond Devos

They say a mime can do anything. It isn't true.
A mime can't do everything. For example,
A mime can't mime someone with nothing to do,
Or rather, someone who is not doing anything,
Which is what my producer asked me to do.
He told me to think about what I had to do,
Which meant I either had to think about doing nothing,
Or I didn't have to think about doing anything.
So I went on stage and began doing nothing,
Or began not doing anything. I'm not sure
Which it was. Paradoxically, the more I did nothing
The more the audience asked each other
What I was doing. They could see I wasn't doing anything,
But wanted to see me do something. The critics,
On the other hand, could see I was doing nothing,
And that I was doing it extremely well.
They didn't expect more, and I couldn't have done less.
Eventually, to please the audience, I made a gesture
Of hopelessness. The producer immediately
Called for the curtain, and started berating me;
Said he'd paid me not to do anything, and I'd done
something,
Which showed I wasn't even good at doing nothing.
Next day the critics didn't write anything,
And since I hadn't done anything, that made us quits.

Noah

As drunk as you can be standing up,
Shirt and face in cherry and white,
His club's colours, he roars for his men:
Go on Glos! Go on! His job is not at risk.
Towards the end of a fierce first half
His look- and sound-alike arrives,
And not a word is said on either side
About the score. His mate asks, *How much
Have they been charging you for a pint then?*
Our man looks down at his glass. *Well I dunno,*
He says, *I've been buying two at a time.*

Nostalgia

Our church clock showed the time in gold
On a black circle, opposite the bus stop
We gathered around as knights to a banner,
Where we learnt patience, in the cold,
And how to hold our water.
The fat boy begged us not
To tickle him, or else he'd burst
Like a bag, and get chapped legs.
As a favour, we kicked him instead.

It was lucky to catch a falling leaf
During the war; it saved a soldier's
Life. But we didn't know the score in peace.
Phillip ran out after a twisting
Sycamore seed and was hit
By an unsuspecting motorcyclist.
That proved there was something in it.

Our bows were made with osier, our arrows
Were the dried stems of goldenrod
With nails in the end for weight.
We wouldn't have harmed a sparrow
But Tommy, the butcher's-boy, aiming high,
Announced that he was going to shoot
God. At which point we all ran away.

A row of unexploded bombs in the clay
Of Barker's field was marked with red flags,
Like an idiot's golf course. All day
We threw stones at them, and fagged
Out, went round to see obliging Tim.

For a penny, he would open
The airing-cupboard door.
For tuppence he'd let you hold them,
The lodger's frost-edged undies,
As soft as a cupped handful of water,
In shimmering, blinding colours.
My little fetishes incubated there.

On the Underground

As the doors began to shut
He launched himself in the air
With a jump of joy that left a cut
And removed a chunk of hair.

He suffered a fall that followed the pride
Of a breathtaking 30-yard dash;
And although his efforts got him inside
It was all a bit too rash.

He struck his head on the rail I was holding,
(I always prefer to stand),
And dropped like a man in a boxing ring
Who's walked into fate's right hand.

He was groaning pitifully, where he fell,
Observed by several ladies.
Did they help him? Did they hell!
He was just as welcome as rabies.

He got up bravely, holding his head,
With blood between his fingers.
They were relieved that he wasn't dead,
And the train didn't have to linger.

This Orpheus found no Euridices
On the Metropolitan line.
His wound would need a dozen stitches,
But that sort of thing takes time.

He lurched to a seat with the obvious lack
Of assistance from those on the train.
But it wasn't shyness holding them back
From consoling the man in pain.

He'd embarrassed them, in a kind of way,
So nobody tried to treat him,
And they couldn't hang about all day;
They were all on their way to meetings.

The only way to catch a train
Is to miss the one before.
That was Chesterton's simple claim,
And advice we shouldn't ignore.

Pantechnicon-van

The almost always unwelcome pantechnicon
Emblazoned with a name and a weak pun
Contains – whichever house it's parked outside –
A room waiting to be taken for a ride,
A chest of drawers in the far interior,
A standard lamp, two shiny leather chairs,
A pink divan and mattress, both upended,
Strapped to the side of the van, now unattended.
A blue and white tea-towel has been dropped
On the tailgate; activity has stopped.
A front door is open, a dustsheet spread
Like ribbed sand over the hall carpet.
But when you return later that afternoon
The street is empty; the giant van has gone,
The entire contents of a house packed in.
They manage it over and over and over again,
The art of preternaturally defying
The laws of space, and energy and time…
Seeing that what needs doing always gets done,
That's the code of the great pantechnicon.

Parts

Hair
It sounds like a discreet
Butler clearing his throat:
A hair. A hair.

A hair is a crack in priceless
Porcelain, a crevasse
On the camera lens.

Hair obscures the worrying headlines
On the brows of readers of *The Times*.

A hair falls on the map
To become an enticing new path,
Leading the hand-picked men
To a dangerous position.

An ingrowing hair
Is the worst kind of traitor,
Climbing the vertebrae
Like insinuating ivy.

What are hairs aerials for?
What do they tell from the stars?
That a head of hair, a fine,
Golden, dandelion sun
Becomes a grey diurnal moon.

Eyes
On the desk is a piece of plain paper.
Two eyes have been stabbed into it
With a pen nib. Between these commas
A funny nose has been drawn, like a drip
That will be caught in the saucer of a mouth.

You will find other marks on the sheet:
Some small amounts badly added up,
Although the figures, in themselves, are neat;
A rough patch where something's been rubbed out,
And a honeycomb of dried coffee-froth.

The desk top is covered with black leather.
If you leave the paper lying where it is,
It's like a chess-board with one white square.
Tomorrow, someone will claim the torn eyes
And hold up the grin on the paper face.

You want to know who it is who's coming?
Good. We like curiosity on this floor.
When you hear movements, knock. Don't go in.
The face will be pushed to you under the door.
A name will be pencilled on it, which you must erase.

Tongue
A stranded pink whale
From seas of tea and beer
The body is its tail
It can say logorrhoea
And other erudite words

It licks the finger that's counting money
Or has been cut opening a can
Laughter and language piggyback on it
Tyrants would have it banned

Feet can stamp on sticks
But cannot stick on stamps
Fingers can unravel string
But cannot sing Ravel
Or tell you to go to hell

Hindus practising yoga
Give it elongating massages
On the banks of the Sacred River
Then use it to block their nasal passages

We never say of our friends
They've got such peculiar tongues
Hers has a sort of bend
His looks more like a stone
Tongues do not tell on their own

A stranded pink whale
With a name like a Chinese dynasty
It loves garlic and snails
And playing with other whales

Arms
Hers was the dirtiest neck I'd ever
Seen, but like unused carbon paper
It had its own kind of clean.

She was the first girl I'd kissed
Improperly: her tongue gave a twist
Like an uprooted carrot. We were up a tree,

Standing on its branches with one
Arm wrapped round the trunk,
Leaving the other hand free to palm

Each other's round parts. It was love,
Precarious and breathless, way above
The sea-level of serious.

And why can't love always be
So, upheld by a huge green tree's
Arms? Write your answer below.

Pet mice

We'd been afraid they'd eat their young,
To save food, or out of jealousy.
But these killings seemed impossible.
Not one creature was left alive,
While everything else looked undisturbed.
How could a murderer have ghosted in
To rip open those soft purses
And scatter their shining jewels around?

I lifted the wooden, home-made box
And the butcher's sawdust ran from the hole –
A mouth with no need to explain.
Hidden there in the chewed-up hessian
Was a torpid rat, fitting its nest
Like a chocolate in a chocolate box.

It must have undermined the cage
Patiently, gnawing at the thick wood
Until its grizzled head could emerge
Like a hunting trophy fallen from the wall.
Then it dragged itself into their world,
Thinking an almost human thought:
Something, perhaps, to do with liberty,
Before setting about them with its teeth.

Picnickers

A shoal of mackerel frittered the sea
Between their titchy island and the shore.
They crouched over their imported business
Of making a fire, and unpacking the picnic,
Weighing some things down with stones
In the wind-attack. Two with nothing to do
Scratched their way up to the high,
Clear space, where small clouds had fallen
On the ground. They could find no water,
Except a reeded puddle of soft mud.
All around a beauty that made them ask
What beauty is, and all around their feet
The small clouds of the dead sheep.

Place for a castle

The barman swears some sailors put RAF
Benevolent Fund lighter-fuel in their drinks,
But nothing in the box. Warships perch
On the horizon, ready to migrate when NATO
Says it's autumn. Holiday-makers empty
Their pockets to find change for the sun.
Yesterday on the pier an old trooper
Sang *Singing In The Rain* in the rain.
If you pass the pier, and follow the beach tents,
As modest as nuns, you come to the sandcastle.

Every day the man rebuilds it, keeping the sand
Moist with a garden spray that says *Psst psst!*
To passers-by. He makes a bob or two.
Not because they reward him for his work.
They aim their money at the barbicans,
The castellated ramparts, and sometimes at him.
He crouches there late into the night,
Sifting coins from the sand, and leaves
A mound that looks a good place for a castle.

Point-to-point

The glazed jockeys have been tipped
From sweetie jars. Their whips

Rat-tat on boots that shine
Like glasses of stout. The urine

From the Gents flows
Down the mouth of a rabbit burrow.

On one sleeve crawls a caterpillar
Like a gooseberry fired through a peashooter.

On the other is a ladybird, so
Bright and intricate; half a tiny tomato.

Nearby, pilgrims went their way
To eat a cake called Canterbury.

I, too, have penitent feet
Crossing the silent grass of the beer tent,

Where a drink has the power of a looking-glass
To raise a hand to the face.

Bitter chalk-dust falls, a shower of time,
Telling the good people to go home.

Denim blue and gaberdine brown
Watch the tents melted down;

Every breast is in its nosebag
And Jill has found her Jag.

Portrait of a gentleman

My dimensions are two
My corners are four,
I am life-size like you
Down there on the floor.

You're seldom more
Alone than in a gallery.
No one looks at you,
Only giant playing-cards
Shuffled and dealt by history.

Beside your shoulder
I see a woman's face
Painted with brushes.
So life-like. Almost one of us.

Looking at art is like a kiss.
It can be done in two ways.
My advice is to look hard, yes,
But also to look softly.

I have been kind to you today.
If I had a banderole it would say
It's rude to stare, now go away.

Railway sleepers

The train departs Cologne on a clear night
For destination Vienna; a change of country
But not vernacular, or gauge. The Rhein in moonlight's
Silver, below high castles like chess-pieces,
Like Black's bishops and rooks.

It's the time to sleep, but it isn't possible.
Mummified in our First Class bunks, with books
And eyes closed, we're fast awake.

Every noise that can be made by metal
Brings us to a stop, close to a speaker
Announcement which means nothing at all.

Below us the lines, and beneath the lines the sleepers,
And while I can't sleep I try to calculate
How many sleepers we've passed over.

At two thousand a mile, I make it a million,
While we lie on narrow platforms,
Heading down the *Eisenbahn*, the Iron Road,
Us nothings, a casual one-off load.

Rain

Rain beat the river to chain-mail.
It rained all that week, all the next.
Behind windows thick with rain
Talk slithered on the surface of silence.
A torrent fanned over common land;
Willows sailed off with tangled rigging,
Centuries of short-cuts drowned.
Weekends shrank to nothing-doing
When it seemed to rain more.
The secateurs, mowers and shears
Became dusted with rust.
The earth gave inch by hesitating
Inch round a citadel of complaint
Where friends billeted from *Riverview,*
Thamesbank and *Ferry Cottage* mooned
Over cups of tea as brown as flood-water.
Their hosts sought corners of their homes
To argue and scold in whispers
Borrowed from the incessant sound of rain.
Tempers grew pencil-sharp, whetted points
In the small pools of their eyes.
Their buried families rolled deep in mud;
Their children wished for each other's deaths.
When the water was dragged away,
It left dwindling pools where fat pike
Threshed under the relentless
Hammering of gulls' beaks.

Remembering my savings stamp

The buff envelope that had its Postage Paid
Was still in my pocket at Waterloo Station
And sent me searching for a post box.

Over fifty years ago, almost on the same spot,
I'd breathlessly licked a savings stamp
And stuck it on the nose of a bomb
Already crusted with different colours.

I couldn't see the point of dropping stamps
On the Germans. If the bomb failed to explode
They'd have my money, and everyone else's,
So they'd be better off. I didn't understand

That by surrendering my savings stamp
I was giving a shilling to the Government
To help the war effort. Lifted up, I gingerly
Patted the metal obelisk three times
And urged by my mother, made a wish.

Rossini, Senior Crescendo

His mother begged him
To make lots of babies,
But he fathered none,

As far as we know.

Van Beethoven urged him
To make lots of Barbers.
In truth, he managed only one.

Senior Crescendo
Had greatness childless;
The Dutchman van Beethoven
Had childless greatness.

Snooker player

He is a general.
He arranges ivory sounds.

He begins by breaking
The symmetry of delta.

He is a general
Who has enemies:
They are colours.

He aims to finish
With an empty field.

Shhh!
He is a general.

The object of his game
Is complete silence.

Snow

Your grave has a white sheet covering it.
When snow last lay so deep, you were alive,
And so much ended here in this pit.
The frosted dwarf-rose branches all contrive
To look like bones; no, worse, look like a hand.
You hated the cold, *The beastly cold,* you'd say,
Rubbing chilblains, twisting the golden band
On your sore, swollen finger, in your way.
Next door, on his allotment, an old man stares
Miserably, as all sentries have stood.
Along the wire fence his dog scatters
Amber beads, the ancient grave-goods,
Reminding me how I tearfully poured away
What was left in your last bottle of whisky.

Some of those handbags are almost human

Ladies' handbags have become more personal,
More precious, more loved.
I sometimes think hearts
Are beating inside their leather skins.
You may see a handbag
But I see a baby chimpanzee
Sitting round-shouldered under the café table
With his thin arms spread on the parquet floor,
Or sidling along the street holding tight
To mother's lowered hand, and when tired
Clinging to her neck, enjoying the ride.
You only have to look at them.
Some of those handbags are almost human.

Stop cock

Drink your beer from a glass
And catch the sweet breath
Of the brewery...

To admire the glow of the barley,
The stalk, ear and whiskers,
The fletched golden arrow...

To catch the scent of hop flowers,
So high on the poles and guy ropes
That men had to clamber on stilts
To pick them...

To see the white lace garter
Slip down the glass,
While all the while...

Your glass of beer's
Sun-shaped surface
Stays perpendicular
To the centre of the Earth.

So drink your beer from a glass.
Drinking out of the bottle
Is like sucking a glass cock.

Strangford, Ulster

At Strangford Lough, or Lough Strangford,
Depending which side you look at it from,
One night, stout-sodden fishermen
Rowed to an island, a piece of Britain

The size of a few tennis courts,
To wipe out a colony of terns.
They trampled eggs and chicks to pulp,
By torchlight, the adult birds screaming

Overhead. Their own mad hard-men
Got wind of this, and there was talk
Of bloody beatings before the gulls
Had finished gorging on the leavings.

In a parable of sorts, the Warden said
That he had seen a jumbo-jet
Of goose-flesh, fuelled on eel-grass,
Take off and head for Greenland,

From Strangford Lough, or Lough Strangford,
Where hope is sold before it's even stolen,
A moth in the mouth of a bat,
In the claws of a late-hunting hawk.

Swimming: 1949

The landing stage was as empty as a slice of bread.
There was no grumbling fisherman, his head
Buried in his tackle-box, picking over things that
He didn't want, wondering where his favourite

Float was, the one made with a porcupine quill
That he'd left behind on the window sill;
No undressed lovers curled up together
Like the pink sausages at the butchers;

No slouching bully waiting to follow
And whip our legs with switches of willow.
We could spend the whole day tossed
Onto the landing stage like beans on toast:

The sons of heroes, who'd been to the cinema
And seen the shark-shaped Spitfire
And the alliterative Hawker Hurricane
Shoot down the evil, lurking German

Bombers. Each of us had a Swiss Roll
Made with a costume and towel,
And pockets full of lucky things –
Feathers from a Jay-bird's wing,

Stones with holes, rusty keys,
Finders-keepers things. All day we
Dived violent-sounding dives: *Belly-flops,*
Dead-man and the leaping, foetal *Bombs.*

Until someone shouted out in fear
When he was grazed by a wooden spear.
Waiting a few feet below the fake,
Reflecting surface was a thick stake,

Now rotted away, planted
Deeply and firmly in the river-bed.
We swam tentatively to the spot
Feeling in murky water for the point,

Then huddled like sweepings on the stage,
Describing all the wounds it could have made,
Doubling up with what looked like laughter
When we imagined the moment after

Our impalement. Having fooled around
So often, we would have found
It funny, a body floating face-down.
We often pretended that we'd drowned.

But I wondered how it was we'd swum
There all summer, and no one
Had died that horrible Vampire's
Death. This was not the past

Banging a broom handle on the ceiling,
Asking us what we were doing
Up there. It was more like
The future greedily thrusting a cocktail-stick

Into a jar full of Maraschino cherries,
But missing. School and the September spiders,
The burst pipes and the blocked drains,
All winter's uncomfortable metaphors, came –

And we never again leapt into strange water.
With sweeping hands, like searching a drawer,
We lowered ourselves carefully in,
For death can be a small thing,
And however safe things may appear,
There's nothing safer than a little fear.

Thames: the upper reaches

Attentive, upright and silent
We glide like statues on a cart
Along a country lane of water.

Dragonflies frisk the air
Between pollarded willows
Whose club-shaped shadows fall
Over fish lazily waving us on.

The sounds of water against the hull
Can be made with your mouth and tongue,
So call it a language if you like.

The sailing boats that reeled and toppled
Like birthday cards on a mantelpiece
Have been left far behind.

Life is narrower and simpler,
The weirs' thundering keyboards
Replaced by placid sluices in braided streams.

We eyes-right in a portrait gallery of cows
Whose hooves have trampled
Uncountable shiny boots
Into the mud at the river's edge.

In pub gardens labradors piss
On beer glasses left on the grass,
And faces looking down from bridges
May smile or yell obscenities.

My spit travels at strolling pace:
If you stirred that white blob
Into all the water in the river
Then filled a glass from it,
It would contain molecules
From the river under my tongue.

Malign fountains of brambles guard their litter,
And Second World War pillboxes squat
Where machine guns would have nested
To defend one of England's fallback positions.
They're protected monuments again.

First prize for names goes to the Windrush,
That beams into the Thames at Newbridge
With gossip from the Cotswolds.
Runner-up is the little river Churn.

Last night the owls discussed who's who.
This morning's mist has turned the river to spilt milk.
The sun blots it up
And is the only light we shall use all day.

Mink nest in rotting flesh
For the hell of it,
Kill everything they can
And move relentlessly on.
The sign they've been around
Is lifelessness, no swimming birds –

But an unexpected comeback of moorhens
Who run for the bus when they see us
Suggests something has changed.
With luck otters are barging in.

Sunlight plays shove-ha'penny
On the water, where a boy
Deftly casts his silver spinner,
A windblown spider, reeling
Out its deceptive thread
To hook and land a cannibal.

We're pushed along
By our own spinning piece of metal
That manipulates the scenery,
While the small passerines of summer
Rehearse in their opera houses.

The banks have set an ambush
Of pelting willows and reeds,
That close in like the brushes of a car wash.

As high and far as we can go,
Our boat has climbed a few hundred feet
Above the first and last lock.
When we turn and head downstream
The map still makes sense, backwards,
Like that near-palindrome
The word *river*.

That time of year

It's that time of year,
When the birds have nothing
To sing for, so go gorging
On elderberries and other fruit,
And garish wounds appear
On cars parked beneath, or near
The high trees in the road.
Violet droppings smear
The car doors, and splashed poppies
Decorate their roofs
Like cheap wallpaper.
It's that time of year.

The air man

I foresee the day when we shall read nothing but telegrams
and prayers.   *Emile Cioran*

A speech on the radio started the war
When our family was on holiday in Cromer
On the unloved North Sea no one
Wants to call their own.

My father's name was Frederick Charles, heir
To another Frederick Charles, who married a
Frederica Carlotta. Their daughter was Freda.
For simplicity's sake he called himself Peter.

Peter was reported missing when I was four
And I've lived more than twice as long as him.
He flew away and never reached the morning.

Counted out the planes like crosses slid
Across the moonlight, silver, cold and liquid,
Planes made from the same materials
As his deck-chair on Cromer beach: metal,

Canvas and wood. Their mission: to lay mines,
'Gardening' in Air Force slang,
Following the navigator's dead-straight lines
Eastward towards the Dogger Bank.

We will never know
What happened to the plane. The radio,
The altimeter, the compass, the speedo
And the crew all headed for zero.

A boxer counted out cannot be counted in;
His name was almost never mentioned again.

My mother hid from thunder
Storms in the airless cupboard under
The stairs where I discovered a banjo with mirror-writing
Showing through the vellum:

Messages, signatures, as if the writers were trapped
Inside the drum,
As if they wished to be remembered
In noise to come.

They included the mothers' names, his and mine,
And a childish drawing of a cocktail glass
In ink faded to the yellow of nicotine,
To the colour of dead grass.

A collapsing silk opera hat
Came to light, an opera hat for what –
For *Die Fledermaus* or doing conjuring tricks?
I found boxing gloves and boots, and hockey sticks.

Everything I know of him was learnt by spying
Or by accident. In his photograph album
A march past of tiny, uniformed men
Keeps on drilling as long as their flag is flying.

Hidden under tea-towels in a kitchen drawer
I unearthed a pair of spectacles and a briar
Pipe, and was told to tell no one.
So this is how I got close to him…

By looking through his glasses blearily,
By sucking bitter air through his pipe,
By shuffling in his boxing boots, so like
The fashionable Converse trainers of today,

And on the banjo, strumming the three
Chords that make musicians
Rich, his initials, F, C and G.

I have whirled round the sun
Over twenty-six thousand times
Since he set off to drop his mines
And I like to think he's still up there,
The air man, a dead man made of air.

The Albatross Coast – La Côte d'Albâtre

At sea, on course for the Alabaster Coast,
For the port the Vikings called *Deep,**
What can you say about the sea
Except that there is nothing to see?

In this English-language brochure
About the Alabaster Coast, its history,
Culture, the countryside, local delicacies,
My eyes fall on one of those literals
That quirkily improve the original.

The translator has accidentally done
What only a practised sculptor can do
With his mallet and his batch of iron tools:
He has changed a kind of stone
In to a kind of bird: Albâtre in to Albatross.

*Dieppe

The bouquet
After Jacques Prévert

What are you doing little girl
With those pretty fresh flowers
Are you going to greet the winner?

What are you doing young lady
With those flowers those wilting flowers
Are you late for the ceremony?

What are you doing woman
With those dried flowers
Have you forgotten the arrangements?

What are you doing old lady
With those dead flowers
Are you waiting for the conqueror?

The cat and the bird
After Jacques Prévert

The village listened miserably
To the wounded bird's cries
It was the only bird in the village
And it was the only cat in the village
That had half-eaten him
And the bird stopped singing
The cat stopped purring
And licking his lips
And the village gave the bird
A marvellous funeral
And the cat who had been invited
Walked behind the little straw coffin
Where the dead bird was laid out
Carried by a pretty young girl
Who couldn't stop crying
The cat said to her
If I'd known how unhappy this would make you
I'd have eaten all of him
And then told you
That I'd seen him fly away
To the very ends of the earth
Too far away to ever return
And you wouldn't be so distraught
So distressed and full of sorrow
Now I see that one should never
Do things by half-measures

The dog's name

A biddable dog, by hearsay,
He badged me in his oily eye,
Ready to be off. Outside the gate
He was running hours late,
So made up time on the track
To the chalk ridge, held back
By a shout, and a louder shout.

But the wind, with a sudden clout,
Blew his name out of my head:
Everything I called instead
Went without any kind of heed.
He parted sheep like a speed-
Boat; wind turfed the crows about,
And I could not call him out

From ransacking the undergrowth
For rabbits. Now we were both
Searching. I yelled every dog's
Name that I could think of,
Running through the alphabet.
Only a feigned turning-back
Set him puzzling, with shouldered stare,

And we both stood frozen there,
About a hundred feet apart,
Waiting for one word to start.
He was halt, I was dumb,
But the name did come,
The revenant dog was claimed,
And we went downhill home again.

The drawer

It opens its mouth wide, the drawer,
Fills lint and cotton-wool lungs before
Exhaling a childhood of aromas:
Iodine, camphor and eucalyptus.

With the stalwart Dettol and Domestos
They always sounded like bold-as-brass
Ancient Romans. Searching for Golden
Eye Ointment, that precious, molten

Balm, I discover creams for burns
And rashes, (good riddance and no returns),
This wrist-strap, for hot sprains,
Buckled on in dressing-up games

By a gladiator or a Robin Hood,
And the soft, leather thumb-guard
That was waggled so suggestively
Behind stiff aunts who came to tea.

Pink soap clatters at the back
But is out-rattled by the black
Bile Beans, the noisiest pills
Ever made. In memory of ills

Of all sorts, I lower my face
Into the drawer, asking for grace
Of some kind, with muffled vows,
My head in a tame lion's mouth.

The great hat race

All participants knew the signal when it came:
A roll of thunder. Off they flew,
At two-thirty precisely. Every man's hat in town
Left its wearer's head, escaped the frown,
To race towards a specified destination –
The statue outside the railway station
Raised to the supreme hero of hats: he
Who invented the Lost Property
Service. (The wind was in on it, had to be.)

Every hat was on the move,
Smart or scruffy, old or new,
All with a handicap and a set of rules,
And differing ideas about how to play it,
How to use the wind, the master of fate,
To their best advantage,
And the bookmakers cried
All hats are off!

A trilby, a racing hat if ever there was one,
Took an early lead.
But there was real class in the field:
Panamas, bowlers, berets, boaters,
Cheese-cutters, a topper, a fez,
Deer-stalkers, and a Breton cap.
The wind was in on it, must have been,
To blow so profusely down every street.

The fez took off fast,
Filled with wind, a bucket of energy,
But he lacked stamina. The beret Basque,
Virtually a frisby in felt, whizzed along
Then pulled a fast one, landing
On his side and rolling at high speed.
The wind was in on it, certainly.

Similarly, the sailor's blanco'd titfer
Wobbled down the high-street
Like a detached hub-cap. But he dropped out
Because this race was a landlubbery thing.
Wind was for lugsails, topsails, staysails
For whistling in shrouds,
For stiffening pennants and flags.
Forget the race, pour me some rum, he said.

A rarity in hattery, but in cricket commonplace,
Was the black bowler, medium pace,
So didn't really stand a chance.
A conjuror's top hat was not allowed
To compete because of the rabbit inside.
With those legs he'd be bound to win,
So they made an official out of him.

The garish schoolboys' caps
Couldn't pass the sweetshop.
No marks for that.
And all over town, hats
Were chasing and racing.
Trilby was still well in the lead.
(The wind was in on it, had to be.)

Fez, in the doldrums, was picked up
By an inventive local beauty
Who used him as a flower-pot
On her sunny balcony:
No happier hat than he.

Balaclava, the murderous bastard,
Was torn to pieces by stray dogs
And nobody cared.
A panama, distracted by a pretty bonnet,
Dropped out of the race at the lady's feet.
She picked him up and handed him to her lover,
Who wears him (another man's hat),
With a smug grin.

Cumbersome homburg, on his way to a funeral,
Almost died from the exertion,
And gave up, on the advice of an American doctor's
Pork pie. Two young toupées, who were disqualified,
Got rather ruffled, and left side by side.
A straw boater was snatched from the air
By a mischievous goose who gave him
To a neighbouring duck to nest in.
Now that is a fulfilled hat.
And all the time, the wind was in on it,
And the hat-band played on.

So who won? You know who won.
The one who won sits on the head of the statue
Outside the railway station.

The guard

William Cobbett, I read,
Scared birds from turnip seeds
And peas at so early an age
That climbing gates and styles
Was a problem. I like
The ambiguity of this note,
And the infinity of doubt.

Was he too small? Sent out
To call, *Away, away, away,*
Take a little bit and come another day,
Great birds, little birds, pigeons and crows,
I'll up with my clappers and down she goes.

The wooden hands caused such fright
The thieves took off and swung like kites
Held by strings of hunger,
Or caught in trees bounding the fields
With eyes as bright as seeds, to wait,
Then slide down the inevitable chute.

But who knows exactly when
Cobbett had this problem?
Perhaps the writer means that he was cursed
In later years for spoiling the birds' feasts;
That as a punishment for being guard
He always slipped back to the ground
When climbing stiles or gates,
His hands wooden, his feet weights.

The Irish fiddler

One of the clichés of the films and theatre
In the days of collars and ties
Was the way a shifty type with something to hide
Would run the first and second fingers of his hand
Around the inside of his shirt collar.

Liam was the sweaty accountant who
Fiddled several thousand pounds
From a man who was my friend, and his;
And Liam did just that, shuffling his fingers round
As if slightly loosening a noose.

The Reverend Robert Walker
skating on Duddingston Loch, by Sir Henry Raeburn

An official sign informed the public
The Victorian section was closed.
All the walls were dark and bare,
Prepared for another kind of painter.
I knew I'd never get so close
Again to seeing the man in black.

Our same Christmas card every year,
Religious only in the sense
It's a reverend gentleman who skates
With folded arms, like a man who waits
For some small, delayed recompense.
Not exactly walking on water,

But as close as he would ever get.
I told the warden I'd come all the way
From London to see my favourite painting,
The Reverend Robert Walker skating;
I was only in Edinburgh for one day,
And I begged the man, begged like a poet.

With a nod he asked me to follow him
Downstairs into the basement,
Where canvases leant in orderly rows
Like corn leaning when the wind blows.
He paced a measurement out then bent
And handed me the frozen frame.

Here was something I hadn't planned,
So I'd only a few minutes to spare
For the most precious thing I'd ever held
Except friends' children, and my own child.
When I arrived, it wasn't there,
Now I was holding it in my hands.

The swan

Seven or eight bright white stars
Wheeling in the heavens
Became in Latin *Cygnus*, the Swan,
That will shine, and has shone
To other parts of the universe –
Not as a constellation of course
But scattered and random.
A pattern needs a name to call it by
As things get lost if they're not named –
For *Cygnus* let us thank mythology
And the imagination of a shepherd-boy.

(There is an asterism in Cygnus –
four stars known as the Northern Cross.)

The tinned scream

The commonest baits were white bread
Kneaded with water to make a grey paste
That finger and thumb rolled into pellets,
Like berries, to hang on the barbed hook,

Or flowerbed worms chopped with scissors
Into smaller worms. But the grown-up bait
Was maggots, found at the angling shop.

I bought a bait-box, a round silver tin
With a perforated lid, and the owner
Spooned them in, like live rice-pudding.
Because of rain, or schoolwork, I forget,
They sat too long on the garage shelf,

And the tin felt strange because it contained
A scream. I prised the lid open and a swarm
Of new-born flies burst out. The dropped tin
Emptied; my awful scream had flown away.

The 218 bus around 1949

We are the boys and girls well known as
Minors of the ABC,
And every Saturday all line up
To see the films we like to shout about with glee...

... were the words we sang, quoted from memory.
Up on the screen a ping-pong ball bounced
From word to word, to help us keep in time,
If not in tune.

The 218 was our red life-line
To the Saturday morning cinema,
Where bandy cowboys in ten-gallon hats
Out-rode and out-drew the unshaved baddies
On ridiculously speeded-up film...

Whereas the vital bus dawdled from stop
To stop between Kingston and Staines.
(Man is born free, but everywhere he is in Staines.)

The conductors' fingers turned perceptibly green
From the copper coins they handled.
Over their serge uniforms they wore
Crossed leather straps, bandito-style:
On one hip a leather pouch
For the pounds, shillings, pence and ha'pennies;
On the other, a ticket-punching machine.

Norman the bully's right hand
Was a face-punching machine.

And the conductors carried a palette
Of pastel-coloured paper tickets
Representing all the different fares.
Each ticket needed a hole punched in it,
Against a specific number,
To show the stop where you should get off.
(One ring on the bell to stop, two to start).

When an inspector climbed on, the fare-dodgers
Tried to sidle past him to the way out,
Which unfortunately was the same as the way in.

And there was no door on that draughty
Class-room, swap-shop, youth-club,
Ghost-train, tunnel-of-love, quiz-show,
Snack-bar, where we dipped our yellowing fingers
In sherbet, and chewed on liquorice wood.

A conductor once materialised
Walking slowly and frighteningly out of fog
Between two headlight fireballs, guiding the driver.
Our poor teeth rattled, and the engine
Made the slow bus shake like a wet dog.
We thought he'd come for our souls.

218's my rhyming-slang for late,
And the later the better, when it comes
For me, and rumbles off to heaven's gate.

We like to laugh and have a sing-song,
Happy boys and girls are we-ee,
We're all pals together,
We're Minors of the ABC.

There are many Niles

Haji Hassan, prince of drivers,
Reminisces about his favourite son,
Light of eye, jewel of heart, and so on,
Then suddenly mad, and dead of rabies.
His sweating passengers are stunned.
In his sadness, Hassan stops to pray,
Conveniently outside his cousin's shop,
Where they all sip coffee grudgingly
And push bargains politely away.

They endure Hassan's conversation,
Silently and uncomfortably, as the road
Jogs them on to Zohser's pyramid,
Which is not a pyramid at all,
But steps to heaven, and from it.
(Gravity, the heart's great enemy,
Will pull it down to a house of dust).

Life is pictured on a piece of stone
Set in a wall of the Queen's tomb:
A hippopotamus gives birth
Into the jaws of a crocodile.
Someone points and asks, *Is this the Nile?*
Haji Hassan, driver of princes, replies:
Nile means water. There are many Niles.

Things undone

Some are remarkable
For what they haven't done.
A friend, as clever as he was tall,
Claimed he'd never scored
A point, a goal, a run
In any kind of sport.
Another, brilliantly self-taught,
Had never in his life owned,
Peddled, ridden or driven
A bike or scooter, motorbike or car,
Or transport of any sort.
One an educator, the other a poet.
If you want to know, both went far.

Thinks bubbles

Rain after a month of drought.
On the path beside the estuary
every pothole is a bowl of water.

One in particular catches the eye,
where bubbles are streaming up
from an underground cavity.

The bubbles form perfect shapes
like polished floating pebbles,
that the breeze rolls aside.

In the puddle, mesmerisingly,
air jets into water, a fountain in reverse,
a fountain in reverse in verse!

Three train journeys

Venice-Milan
I worried all the way from cold Venice
To wet Milan: on the reserved seat beside me
Sat a neat parcel, placed by an elegant lady
Who stood in the corridor with a sad face.

She prevented other passengers using this seat,
Although there was only standing room
From Verona onwards. I thought it was a bomb;
That was all I could think, but dared not say it.

The ticket-inspector was as puzzled as us.
He identified the owner; a muffled conversation,
Some glances, shrugs. He nodded and moved on.
When she retrieved the package, the nervous

Compartment relaxed. I've thought it over for years,
And believe she was taking her dear husband's remains
On their last journey, to Milan by train,
Standing in the corridor, hiding her tears.

London-Edinburgh
Going up on the night-train
For the rugby, with a pack of cards
And crates of Ben Truman. Poker, jokes
And beer all night, through blackened
England, in a fog of cigarette smoke:
A minor party of the slightly damned.

Smudged, rank, with thick voices,
We sneaked up to bathrooms
In the granite North British Hotel

To shower and shave – went down
To breakfast, with whisky in our coffee,
And whisky in our porridge.
There was consternation when a vicar
Was found dead in a cubicle
In the Gentlemen's. A voice said
I wonder if he's got a ticket on him?
Shocked silence, redeemed by,
A ticket to heaven I mean.

Paris-Marseilles
To indulge Patrick's fear of flying
(A vain, spoiled, rude, stupid lout
With an inexplicable dislike of food)
We took the TGV from Paris to Marseilles,
En route to the worst holiday of our lives:
Days of malice and sulks, not helped
By the shifty actor, inheritance-hunting
From a French uncle conveniently nearby,
Or Patrick's plastic girl-friend, with pop-music
Plugged in her ears, deaf to all greetings
And courtesy. We lied an excuse and retreated
To Paris, to people having conversations.

The best bit was on the journey down
When a shih-tzu on a yellow lead, held
By a smiling woman, sauntered into the bar,
Paused, looked, and shat on Patrick's shoes.
The owner wafted a paper serviette
From the counter, and nonchalantly cleaned up
Some of the mess, before turning away
To order a glass of champagne. Clever dog!
And he without a word of French to complain.

To Mr. Hudgell, at *May Cottage*

Mr. Hudgell, I'm at your ever-green gate,
Where your son Phillip and I used to wait
For any girl who came by, *Like tomcats,*
Said Mr. Griffin the grocer, but his kindly, fat

Wife, who swept the pavement, sold us broken
Biscuits for threepence a bag to eat in our den,
Sitting on boxes of Clayton's Lemonade,
Ginger Ale, and Soda Water. You made

Your living as a rep., cycling to distant pubs,
Peddling soft-drinks; took your golf clubs
By train to your sister's at Cromer every year.
A dapper, handsome widower, looming on posters

For Mannikin Cigars, looking every inch a gent,
You played the same part in life: but never went
For drinks or dinner at the village's friendly homes.
You kept to your gentlemanly self, forever known

As *Mister* Hudgell, mourning your dear, skeletal
Wife, who you always described as *a perfect angel.*
She could not live to see lovely daughter Jane
Modelling for *Vogue*; or laughing Phyllis, plain,

But more fun than a fairground, become an idol
To us desperate boys, quite insufferable
Because her boyfriends had to win us over
To stay in the running as serious Phyllis-lovers.

We made their sex-lives difficult, always around
When, sinking hand-in-hand, they thought they'd found
A hidden spot in the park. No point in threats;
Only dollops of cash, or a pack of cigarettes

Bought the longed-for fumbling in privacy:
Never what the *News of the World* called *intimacy*.
We were unlovable, nevertheless loved.
We explored your wardrobe; gingerly passed round your hoard

Of Johnny Walker whisky, your heavy revolver,
(Service issue for an officer in the Great War),
And the loose bullets. Hidden by net curtains,
At the upstairs front window, we had uncertain

Fun blowing mouthfuls of stinging pearl-barley
Through the long, glass tubes needed for accuracy –
From a chemist's in Staines; the sharp, cut ends
Rounded-off in a gas flame. Some friends

Guessed, but passers-by never discovered
The origin of this shower from overhead.
But now we had found real, live ammo,
Pip had a typical idea; and wouldn't you know,

It meant shooting Mr. Griffin's pigs next door.
One of the brass cartridges was wedged in a fork
Of your apple tree, aimed at his makeshift sty.
From the back bedroom, with Pip's air-gun, we tried

To hit the firing-cap. Incredibly, the sixth
Shot did it. Mr. Griffin's huffing pigs
Huffed on. God knows where the lethal bullet
Went. Pearl-barley wasn't the same after that;

We ceased fire with primitive glass blowpipes.
You read my first poem; helped me type
It in black, and red, on your machine; let me write
Letters with your new Biro. The very sight

Of it writing upside down brought neighbours
To your house. We polished your shoes out-of-doors,
Sitting by the lily-of-the-valley border; picked
Your blackcurrants, mowed the lawn, got ticked-

Off for beheading border plants besides.
You were strict, fair and kind; always dignified,
And unmanfully tactful. You introduced me
To some arriving, grown-up mysteries:

Shaving, when not to laugh, cutting cigars,
How to sponge and press a pair of weary trousers,
How to carve well, and sharpen the carving knife;
To be brave, watching you lose your vanishing wife.

Your books were open to me, there for loan:
A Boots Library. In a cold room at home
We had some solid collections, like Shakespeare,
Great Short Stories of the World, on thinnest paper,

The thrilling, drum-beating poems of Rudyard Kipling,
And *Great Poems of the World.* Time-consuming
Stuff. You insisted I should read Somerset
Maugham's short stories; somewhat watchfully let

Me pour over your treasured, bound editions
Of *Punch,* (Hands washed under supervision),
With a glass of 'pop' on the carpet in your parlour.
You had the first television our gang ever saw.

As we gawped at the Interlude, an idling swan,
God Bless! You said; drove us out for the afternoon,
To look for something interesting to do.
I'm at your gate, Mr. Hudgell, to *say, Thank you.*

**To the red wine stains on the table cloth
in a French restaurant (1936)**
After Karl Zuckmayer

You catch my eye as I sit down alone
And shove the plate that was hiding you away.
My first swig's to the men and women unknown
Who drank wine at this grubby table today

And scattered my place with golden crumbs of bread.
The talk's as colourful as bright refracted light,
For this is the land of the must-be-seen-and-heard,
Where sometimes God himself stays up all night.

I lay on your soil, in pain, and terrified,
In a world shredded by steel and drenched in blood.
Perhaps the soldier who nearly shot me dead
Is the smiling waiter bringing me my food.

I have tasted the bitter tears of this land,
Where I was certain I was going to die.
Dear country, I bow stiffly, take your hand,
And kiss the specks of blood and wine goodbye.

Wine spurts from the muzzle as the waiter pours;
It's hit and miss, so drink up table-cloth.
This foreigner must depart, as the light withdraws,
To the forests and the grey fogs of the North.

Trotting races at Portbail

On the far side of the municipal race track
Good-natured horses from the local riding school
Graze in persistent drizzle. Clouds stacked
Over the Atlantic advance, while water pools
Around our boots. On to the scene trot sleek
Racehorses, harnessed to sulkies, their drivers in silk.

The loose horses gather by the rail and wait.
When a race passes, stirred by the elegant few,
The many gallop beside them – but concentrate,
Concentrate's what trotters have to do.
If they break into a gallop, disqualification
Is promptly announced on the loudspeaker system.

So attention from off-duty horses is unwelcome,
Who saunter across their field to position A,
Ready to join in more informal fun,
And give the groomed visitors a run for their money.
It's an interesting sideshow, watching instinct prevail
In an impromptu herd divided by a rail.

Two ponds

Jim Hetherington's pond

Jim grubbed out the hole
To stock with a pudding of spawn
From a pond in the hills. He stretched netting
Across to deter predatory birds.

Creator and protector, every frog
That crawls from near or far to the mating ritual
Is one of his originals, or a descendant,
Born in his pond, courtesy of his jam jar.

Now and then a frog swims clear
Of the imbricate, groaning, incestuous
Stew and looks up with goo-goo eyes
At their God surveying
The antics in their muddy little O,
As if to say, *We're doing this for you.*

John Leach's pond

A hired man in a yellow JCB
Excavated John's wintering field in a week.
He ripped up truck-loads of Somerset turf and
Shrubs but avoided the staked area, the island-
To-be. Keeping the pond brim-full was easy:
John diverted a stream the monks at Muchelney
Abbey had dug, and filled the hole with holy water.

That first spring a pair of swans caught a
Glimpse of the pond and glided down for a closer look
(Tenants with royal connections, who'd go by the book).
They paddled the new water and paced
Out the island, the perfect nesting place.

The pottery oven raged in its brick cage, fed
Wood though a true hell-hole, and red-
Faced we ate stew from bowls made by John,
And drank cider from mugs he'd thrown.
Concerning the pond, I overheard John say,
It's the best thing I've ever made in clay.

Two winds

Two winds that will never meet
Share the narrows of our street.

Which wind is on its way,
Which wind will come today?

One works hard, the other plays –
Rattles the letter-box, runs away,

Then piles leaves against the door
That charge like soldiers over the floor.

A whiff of logs the neighbours burn
Announces the other wind's return,

And a cold reception is abroad
When this one comes to sweep the road.

Which wind will blow today,
Which wind is on its way?

Will the children have to stay
Indoors, or can they go and play?

Where do the cats face on the fence,
Is it Cromer or Penzance?

I've just heard the church clock chime,
So I know the wind, and know the time.

Under the hosepipe

Not the purposeful beginning
Clamped to a shiny faucet,
The pipe stiffening from water pressure,
The glorious ending in a mythical rainbow
Woven into spray. That's not it.

Life is the dun loops where the hosepipe lay,
More a diagram of convulsions,
Or the result of a disembowelment,
Than a rudimentary alphabet.
In place of a hope-bringing message,
There's forgotten yardage, winding
To the black, neatly-dug hyphen
Where the coffin comes to rest.

Under the hosepipe, no love.
In it, no life. Nothing grows on it.
After it has passed the last tear
A worm enters the nozzle, to fatten,
And stretch, cast off its rubber coat,
And glistening, straited, suck at the tap.

Virgin and child

The young woman modelling the Virgin
Is given one impossibly beautiful breast,
And another, smaller, tucked up under her arm.
(This way the medieval sets us tests.)

A small businessman sits on her knee in thought.
Poor guileless thing, she turned the royal head;
Poisoned, she died while carrying her fourth
Royal bastard; two days on her deathbed!

Her tomb was desecrated, and a tenth of her
Remains were found in an ordinary pigsty:
Bone, skin, muscle and pubic hair –
Hair that was hers, incontestably.

Saint Joan, a contemporary, fared worse than that.
Her ashes, authenticated by papal commission,
Proved those of an Egyptian mummy and a cat,
Not the bones the English soldiers pissed on.

White-ribbon day

A map of blood is drying on
Mercator's neat paving stones.
Yards of regulation ribbon
Looped around a litter bin
'Seal off' in inverted commas
This part of the slaughter house.

Today is a white-ribbon day
For the man who's gone away;
Now his name will have to be
Tipp-Exed off the stationery.
White is sad, and always has been,
Since the first dropped ice-cream

Lying there so far below
On our new and roomy shoes.
And all the time we walk and talk
Our feet are wearing through to chalk,
Leaving on the springing green
A ribbon showing where we've been.

Wicket-keeper

Our wicket-keeper had a weak bladder
But gulped beer as gladly as air;
Was always last to take the field,
Adjusting his protective shield,
Muttering *LBW mate,*
Which meant, *Let the Buggers Wait.*
He disliked the Batting Class,
And while they carefully took their guard,
Knelt down in sarcastic prayer,
And hummed off each departing player
With the *Dead March* from *Saul.*
Contemplating the next ball
The calmest batsman, thumb in belt,
Flinched at his deliberate belch,
Or he'd creep up close behind
If he felt like breaking wind.
He took his pisses in the ditch
At the cemetery end of the pitch
When a convenient wicket fell,
And if he couldn't wait just held
Things up. He was never quick,
But one day, there on the rec,
He left his padded gloves lying
Near the stumps, like some dying
Bird, and what we saw and heard
Was horrifying – the sudden scared
Shout, the long scream choked
Off, the billowing yellow smoke
Torn through with a claw of flame.
Naturally, we abandoned the game.
All we found in the scorched bushes
Was a seething pile of ashes.
But his gloves still hang in the bar,
Over the fireplace, unclaimed so far.

World War One

they opened the sluices at nieuport on the command of the king and ypres town was at sea level wasnt it so the germans nabbed all the high ground early on we called fifty feet a ridge and a hundred and fifty a hill thats what we fought for ridges and hills so wed capture a salient then get thrown off then back wed go one hill we held only for the weekend like we were just looking after it as you can imagine the millions of shells we fired at fritz and the millions of shells fritz fired at us destroyed the drainage systems there was once we couldnt dig in because of the rain and mud so what we did was we stood there all night with the darkness our only protection in one attack the hun advanced with a drummer no you honestly cant believe it and no one shot at him but that was early on the commonest death was mostly a bullet or shrapnel wound where you fell into the mud and drowned in a few minutes water rats made homes in decomposed bodies when the first gas came they told us to piss on our handkerchiefs and hold them over our mouths it did no good and not against the flame throwers either but goodbye to all that plus a shilling a day which was a lot when you were seventeen just remembered we rescued this german officer whose leg was gone and the way he felt around in his pocket you could tell he was looking for a present for us like a kind of tip and finally he handed me three lumps of sugar soaked in his blood which we just chucked away it's a good job we won when you think about it

Written in my room

My bed-sitting room up the first stair
Was exactly level with the upper deck
Of the 52 bus when it stopped square
Outside, on the way to Victoria Station.

With a re-cycled shilling for the meter
The gas fire glowed with five gold bars,
In the cosiest room in West Eleven.

I lent the room to two friends.
One wrote and planted a fanciful letter
From the girl he'd taken into my bed,
Saying he had been a wonderful lover.

Tranquility was what another wanted,
Somewhere to work on his early plays.

From the one hand came a fake note,
From the other, writing that led the way
To *The Accrington Pals* and *The Herbal Bed,*
Which takes me back to where I started.

Richard Gordon-Freeman was born in Chester in 1938. His father was an RAF bomber pilot, killed in action in '42. His mother became a teacher.

His childhood was spent at Laleham-on-Thames, and he was fortunate to obtain a Middlesex County Council grant to board at Mill Hill School from 1951-56.

Exempt from National Service, having badly broken a leg playing rugby, he went to Germany for a working holiday and stayed a year-and-a-half, to learn the language.

On his return, he got a job as a copywriter with the London advertising agency, C. D. Notley, where he shared an office with Assia Wevill, wife of the Canadian poet David Wevill. The poets Peter Porter, Oliver Bernard, Edward Lucie-Smith and, briefly, Peter Redgrave worked there, as well as the novelist William Trevor. Bernard Gutteridge and Gavin Ewart were employed just round the corner at another advertising agency, J. Walter Thompson.

In this impressive company, he started writing poetry, which first appeared in *Ambit*. He published *Graffiti* (Hutchinson) in 1968, an attractive book on the subject which was well reviewed.

The advertising business took him to the Far East for nearly two years. Then, back in the UK, he became a freelance writer, mostly providing scripts for documentary films. This led to establishing a film production company, based at Shepperton Studios.

After several enjoyable years in the business, he now follows a variety of interests; writing, painting, and studying the Stone and Bronze Age cultures of Western Europe.

Richard has always felt a particular dislike for the *Big Steamers* in the arts (see below), who persist in telling us how uncivilised we are, while quietly pocketing large sums of our money. He, on the other hand, would like to thank everyone who ever paid him for doing anything.

('Big Steamers': From Rudyard Kipling's line 'Oh, where are you going to, all you big steamers').

Other books by the author:

The Rain that Eats (Arts Printing, Malaysia)
Graffiti (Hutchinson)
The Dog's Name (privately published)
Le or La – How to Remember the Genders of French Nouns (Packard)
A Letter to the Alphabet (privately published)